FINANCIAL LITERACY FOR TEENS AND YOUNG ADULTS

The Money Mindset for Teens and Young Adults to Attain Financial Well-being

James Edwards

TABLE OF CONTENTS

INTRODUCTION

Every young person needs to be able to maneuver the complex world of personal finance in today's fast-paced, globally connected world. Yet, traditional education frequently ignores the route to financial wisdom. It seems like we should be able to manage money like financial experts overnight without any help. 'FINANCIAL LITERACY FOR TEENS AND YOUNG ADULTS: The Money Mindset for Teens and Young Adults to Attain Financial Well-being' can be useful in this situation.

This book, written especially for young people anxious to safeguard their financial future, is your compass to the fascinating world of financial literacy. This thorough guide will help you understand and confidently manage your finances whether you're a young professional just starting out on your own, a college graduate, or a high school student.

'FINANCIAL LITERACY FOR TEENS AND YOUNG ADULTS' tackles a wide range of financial topics in an approachable and entertaining way, from making a budget to comprehending credit scores, from saving and investing sensibly to paying off student loans. We'll demystify finance so that young readers can understand it and enjoy it without being overtaken by technical terms or intricate financial ideas.

This book seeks to equip you with the knowledge and skills necessary to make wise financial decisions, steer clear of common pitfalls, and lay a solid foundation for a prosperous future. It's about building the life you want and deserve, not just about handling money.

So come along for the ride if you're prepared to take charge of your financial future. 'FINANCIAL LITERACY FOR TEENS AND YOUNG ADULTS' will provide you with the information, abilities, and self-assurance you need to create a safe and prosperous financial future. Together, we can make your money work for you and realize your aspirations. This is where your financial journey begins.

CHAPTER ONE

The Importance of Financial Literacy for Teens and Young Adults

Envision setting out on a road trip without a map, GPS, or knowledge of where you're going. You have a car, fuel, and the desire to explore, but you are missing some vital equipment to accomplish your aim in a safe and efficient manner. This scenario may seem unbelievable, but it's a reality for many teenagers and young adults who are attempting to navigate the difficult world of personal finance without the necessary financial literacy.

We'll look at the relevance of financial literacy for teens and young adults in this chapter. We'll talk about how it affects you now and in the future, emphasizing the various ways it can help you make wise financial decisions, steer clear of common pitfalls, and accomplish your objectives in life.

1. Freedom and Economic Independence

Economic independence is predicated on having sound financial knowledge. You're slowly making your way into the world of financial responsibility as a young adult or adolescent. This is the period of time when you begin to make financial decisions that will affect you for the rest of your life, such as budgeting and earning. Financial literacy gives you the ability to manage your finances, become less dependent on other people, and make decisions that are consistent with your objectives and values.

2. Establishing a Safe Future

The goal of financial literacy is to secure your future, not just your present. It's important to understand the ideas behind investing, saving, and retirement planning if you want to live a worry-free and comfortable retirement. Because of the miracle of compound interest, the earlier you begin saving and investing, the more time your money has to grow.

3. Escape Debt Traps

Youth who lack financial literacy are more likely to get absorbed into the debt cycle. When used responsibly, credit cards, loans, and other forms of borrowing can be useful tools; however, if they are handled improperly, they can quickly become burdensome. You can avoid building up uncontrollable debt and manage credit responsibly if you have a solid financial education.

4. Making Wise Financial Decisions

You have to make financial decisions all the time in today's world, from picking a bank account to buying stocks. Being financially literate gives you the power to evaluate situations critically and make wise decisions. It assists you in making decisions that are in line with your short-term and long-term goals, interpreting complicated financial jargon, and appreciating the advantages and disadvantages of various options.

5. Improving Career Opportunities

Your career prospects may also be impacted by your level of financial literacy. Financial responsibility and money management abilities are highly valued by employers in their workforce. You might find yourself more desirable to employers if you can prove that you're responsible and wise with money.

6. Overcoming Financial Difficulties

Financial literacy serves as your safety net in life's unpredictable turns. Being financially prepared may mean the difference between surviving a medical emergency, having your car fixed, or experiencing an unexpected job loss.

7. Comprehending Economic Frameworks

It is your duty as a responsible citizen to be somewhat informed about the operation of the economy. Being financially literate helps you see the bigger picture of the economy, which is helpful when assessing government policies, comprehending the effects of inflation, or taking part in conversations about economic matters that impact your nation and community.

8. Promoting Your Dream of Entrepreneurship

To launch a side project or launch your own business, you must be financially literate. It gives you the tools to access capital, handle your company's finances, and make wise financial decisions to support your entrepreneurial pursuits.

In summary, financial literacy is an important life skill that can have a huge impact on your future and general well-being. It empowers you to secure a better life for your family and yourself, develop economic independence, and make wise financial decisions. You can use the information you learn about money management, investing, saving, and staying out of debt as a compass to help you achieve both financial success and personal fulfillment. You will acquire insightful knowledge and useful guidance throughout this book that will assist you in acquiring financial literacy abilities that will serve you well for the rest of your life.

CHAPTER TWO

Mastering Money: What It Is and How It Functions

Money is an incredibly potent tool that influences nearly every facet of our lives, including the opportunities available to us and the way we live and work. We'll delve into the basic ideas of money in this chapter, explaining what it is, how it functions, and why it's important to understand.

Money: What Is It?

We can define money in accordance with its basic functions for mankind, and it serves as a means of exchange, an entity of account, and a stock of price.

1. Medium of Exchange: The intermediary in business dealings is money. It is something you offer in return for products or services. Consider this: money can be used to facilitate trade in place of bartering or exchanging one item for another. It makes transactions far easier and more adequate.

2. Unit of Account: Money offers a standard way to gauge the worth of goods and services. We understand the value of anything we say costs $10 in relation to other items priced in the same currency. This standardization facilitates our comprehension of prices and aids in our ability to make wise financial decisions.

3. Store of Value: Funds can be invested in or saved for later. It retains its value over time, enabling you to postpone making purchases or make long-term plans. This function is critical for saving, investing, and accumulating wealth.

The Evolution of Money

Money has an interesting and long history. It has evolved over the centuries to reflect the needs and preferences of various societies. Let us look at some of the major turning points in the evolution of money:

1. Barter System: Prior to the invention of money, people relied on barter, in which they directly exchanged goods and services. This system had limitations because it required a double coincidence of wants - you had to find someone who wanted what you had to offer while also having something you wanted in return.

2. Commodity Money: Commodity money emerged as societies became more complex. This was money that was backed by a valuable commodity like gold, silver, or cattle. Because these commodities had intrinsic value, people accepted them as payment.

3. Fiat Money: The majority of money in circulation today is fiat money. It has no intrinsic value and is not backed by anything tangible. It is accepted instead because the government declares it a legal tender. Fiat money's value is determined by trust and faith in the issuing authority.

4. Digital Money: In today's world, digital money is increasingly supplementing physical cash. The majority of transactions take place electronically, with money stored digitally in bank accounts and payment systems.

The Function of Money

It's important to understand how money functions if you want to manage your finances well. The following concepts are necessary to comprehend in order to master how money functions:

1. Currency: The majority of nations have bank deposits and physical currency in the form of bills and coins. Whereas bank deposits are kept electronically in a bank account, currency is what you carry in your wallet.

2. Inflation: Over time, the cost of goods and services will gradually rise due to inflation. Money loses purchasing power as a result of this. Either you must invest sensibly or earn interest for your money to retain its value.

3. Banks: Within the financial system, banks are essential. They handle transactions, pay interest on deposits, store your money, and offer loans. Financial literacy requires knowing how banks work and how to use their services.

4. Budgeting: Making a budget enables you to effectively manage your finances. It entails monitoring your earnings, outlays, and savings objectives. You can plan for your financial future and prevent overspending by using a budget.

5. Investing: Over time, investing helps your money grow. You can increase your wealth by investing in a variety of securities, including stocks, bonds, real estate, and mutual funds. But there are risks associated with investing, so it's critical to comprehend these risks and make wise choices.

Why Is Money Important?

Money is a tool that allows you to achieve your dreams and live a happy life. It offers security, liberty, and opportunities. Making the most of your money requires financial literacy, which begins with understanding what money is and how it works.

In the following chapters, we'll go over various financial topics in greater depth, from earning and saving to investing and debt management. You'll be better equipped to make informed financial decisions and build a secure financial future if you have this knowledge. So, let us continue on our financial literacy journey!

CHAPTER THREE

Defining Your Financial Goals and Preferences

People do not achieve financial independence and security by chance. They are the result of clearly defined financial objectives and priorities. This chapter will discuss the importance of defining your financial goals, developing a plan to achieve them, and making wise decisions along the way. You'll be well on your way to making your financial dreams a reality by the end of this chapter.

The Power of Financial Goals

Goals give your financial life meaning and purpose. They act as a guidebook to help you maneuver the vast landscape of personal finance. Setting clear and specific financial goals increases your chances of staying motivated, making better decisions, and tracking your progress.

Different Types of Financial Goals

1. Short-Term Goals: These are objectives you want to accomplish in the near future, usually within a year. Saving for a new smartphone, paying off a small debt, or establishing an emergency fund are some examples.

2. Medium-Term Goals: These objectives have a time frame of 1 to 5 years. They could include saving for a vacation, purchasing a car, or paying for college.

3. Long-Term Goals: Long-term goals span more than five years and frequently revolve around major life events such as homeownership, retirement, or starting a family.

4. Lifestyle Goals: These objectives reflect your desired standard of living. They include things like a nice home, travel, hobbies, and leisure.

5. Financial Independence Goals: These objectives center on attaining stability and financial independence. They entail increasing wealth, lowering debt, and safeguarding your future financial well-being.

SMART Objectives For Understanding Goal-Setting

One common method for creating goals is to apply the SMART criteria:

Each letter of the word 'SMART' applies to the understanding of goal-setting.

S stands for Specific

M stands for Measurable

A stands for Achievable

R stands for Relevance

T stands for Time-bound

a. Specific: Clearly state your objectives. Say something like, "I want to save $1,000 for a vacation within the next 6 months," as opposed to, "I want to save money."

b. Measurable: Quantify your objectives. You ought to be able to monitor your advancement. A goal should have the quantity of a thing that's desired and the time interval for obtaining it. A good example is considering that you will save $300 every month for the next four months.

c. Achievable: Make sure your objectives are doable given your existing financial circumstances. Frustration can result from establishing an unreasonable goal.

d. Relevant: Your objectives ought to be commensurate with your life and financial circumstances. It's important that you consider the things that are most relevant to you.

e. Time-bound: Give your objectives a due date. This gives you a sense of urgency and aids in keeping you on course.

Setting Financial Priorities

While it would be ideal to accomplish all of your financial objectives at once, you might have to set priorities in the real world. This is how you do it:

1. Determine Your Values: Consider the things that are most significant to you. Is it preparing for a cozy retirement? Repaying your education loans? Launching a company on your own? Identifying your core values will assist you in setting your priorities.

2. Take Urgency Into Account: Some objectives, such as paying off high-interest debt, might need to be attended to right away. Give these objectives top priority over those that can wait.

3. Assess Risk: Consider the benefits and risks connected to each objective. For instance, there may be greater risk involved in long-term stock market growth investments than in short-term vacation savings.

4. Financial Impact: Take into account the impact each goal will have on your overall financial health. Give top priority to objectives that will improve your financial situation.

5. Resource Availability: Evaluate the resources you have available, such as your time, money, and savings. Set priorities for the things you can afford to do.

6. Establish a Hierarchy: After taking these things into account, arrange your objectives into a hierarchy. Proceed down the list, starting with the most crucial items.

Formulating A Financial Plan

Now that you have prioritized and established your goals, it is time to make a financial plan to get there. A financial plan is similar to a road map that shows you how to get where you want to go. The following are essential steps to create your plan:

1. Budget: Make a spending plan that accounts for your earnings, outlays, and savings. This will assist you in allocating your funds to your objectives.

2. Savings and Investments: Ascertain the amount of savings required for every objective and select suitable savings or investment instruments.

3. Debt Management: Make a plan to pay off any debts you may have. Give high-interest debts a top priority in repayment.

4. Emergency Fund: Establish an emergency fund to safeguard your goal-achieving progress and pay for unforeseen costs.

5. Regular Monitoring: Check your financial plan on a regular basis to make sure you are on track and make necessary adjustments.

The Necessity of Patience

It's important to keep in mind that attaining financial objectives requires patience and self-control. You should not despair when you do not obtain the result you seek at once. It's important to understand that the way forward is to keep trying until you achieve the result you seek. If you stick to your plan, eventually your efforts will be rewarded.

This chapter has covered the importance of establishing specific financial objectives, how to rank them, and how to create a financial plan. You can achieve financial success and lay a strong foundation for your future by implementing these principles into your financial life.

CHAPTER FOUR

Budgeting: Your Guide to Financial Success

Understanding how to manage your money is a necessary skill that can lead to financial success. Money is a very effective tool. This chapter will go over budgeting, which is similar to having a financial road map. A budget, like a route plan, helps you allocate your financial resources when planning a road trip. It is an important tool for teens and young adults to establish a solid financial foundation.

Understanding Budget

A budget is a financial plan that outlines your expenditures. It supports your decision-making regarding investments, savings, and expenditures. Consider it a roadmap that outlines the most effective path to reaching your financial objectives. You can make your money work for you and prevent financial stress by making and adhering to a budget.

Why Is a Budget Necessary?

1. Track Your Money: You can better understand where your money is going and where it's coming from by using a budget. Knowing how much money you have and where it's going will help you make wise financial decisions.

2. Set Financial Goals: You can prioritize and set financial goals when you have a budget. A budget assists you in allocating funds to reach your objectives, such as saving for college, a new video game, or a bike.

3. Restrict Your Spending: It's easy to go overboard with unnecessary purchases when you don't have a budget. A budget helps you control your spending and prevents both buyer's regret and impulsive purchases.

4. Be Ready for Emergencies: Unpredictability is a part of life, and emergencies like unplanned medical expenses or auto repairs can occur. Creating an emergency fund with a budget allows you to deal with unforeseen expenses without incurring debt.

How to Make a Budget

1. Income: Begin by enumerating every penny you consistently receive. This could be gifts from family members, money from part-time work, or an allowance. This is what you make.

2. Expenses: The next thing is for you to enumerate every expense you have. Expenses fall into two categories: necessities and wants. Needs such as clothing, food, school supplies, and transportation are necessary expenses. Desires are things you'd like to have but don't need, like eating out or the newest technology.

3. Savings and Goals: Establish your goals and the amount of money you wish to save. Make a budget and set aside money for things like college or a new gaming system.

4. Establish Your Budget: Take your entire spending out of your income. You can save the remaining amount or use it toward other financial objectives. You will need to reduce your non-essential spending if your expenses exceed your income.

Budgeting Tips

1. Set priorities: Ensure that your needs take precedence over your wants. Your budget should always account for your needs.

2. Save First: At the start of every month, allocate funds to your savings and financial objectives. This guarantees that you are investing in your future rather than squandering money on items you might later regret.

3. Monitor Your Spending: Make a note of every penny you spend each day. It will make it simpler for you to follow your budget and help you see where your money is going.

4. Be Adaptable: Since life is unpredictable, it's acceptable to make necessary adjustments to your budget. If you receive additional funds, such as a gift, think about investing or saving rather than squandering it all.

In summary, creating a budget is like having a treasure map that points the way to financial success. It supports goal-setting, financial management, and readiness for life's uncertainties. Developing a solid foundation in budgeting when you're a teen or young adult will benefit you in the long run. Thus, begin now, and as you create and adhere to each budget, watch as your financial future becomes increasingly brighter.

CHAPTER FIVE

Savings and Banking

We will delve into the realm of banking and saving in this chapter. An important aspect of financial literacy is knowing how banks operate and how to manage your finances. Understanding the ins and outs of banking and saving can put you on the road to financial success, regardless of your age — whether you're a young adult trying to secure your future or an adolescent starting your first job.

Definition of A Bank:

A bank is a type of financial institution that provides various services to assist you in managing and increasing your savings. A bank's primary duties include keeping your money safe, lending it to others, and enabling transactions. Commercial banks, savings banks, credit unions, and Internet banks are among the various kinds of banks. Every kind of bank has unique benefits and drawbacks in addition to providing a variety of services.

Bank Account Types

Banks provide a range of account kinds, each intended for a particular use. Here are a few typical bank account types:

1. Savings Account: This is a simple account that gives you the chance to save money and get a little interest. It's an excellent spot to begin saving money.

2. Checking Account: Daily activities such as making purchases and paying bills are done through a checking account. Debit cards are often included with checking accounts so you can easily access your money.

3. Certificate of Deposit (CD): The third type of savings account is a certificate of deposit (CD), which has a set term and interest rate. In return for a higher interest rate, you promise not to take the money out for a predetermined amount of time.

4. Money Market Account: Generally offering higher interest rates than standard savings accounts, this kind of account might have limitations on how many withdrawals are allowed.

5. Individual Retirement Account (IRA): An IRA is a long-term retirement savings account that offers tax advantages. Traditional and Roth IRAs are available, and each has unique tax advantages.

How Banks Earn Income

Banks make money by lending it to others and collecting interest in addition to simply holding your money. The bank uses the money you deposit in a savings account to lend money to people and businesses. The bank makes money when they charge borrowers more in interest than they pay you. To entice deposits and use them for lending, is one of the reasons they offer interest on your savings.

How to Open a Bank Account

You may be required to present identification when opening a bank account, such as a passport or driver's license, as well as occasionally proof of address. Make sure you are aware of the account's fees as well as any minimum balance requirements.

Mobile and Internet Banking

Many banks allow you to manage your accounts, pay bills, and transfer money from your computer or smartphone via their online and mobile banking services. Although these tools can be very useful, you need to exercise caution when it comes to privacy and security.

Monitoring Your Bank Transactions

It's critical to monitor your bank statements. It supports you in keeping an eye on your expenditures, verifying that no unauthorized transactions have taken place and that your account balance is correct. In order to assist you in keeping track of your finances, many banks also provide apps and alerts.

The Value of Saving

One essential financial habit is saving. It helps you reach your objectives, offers a safety net for unforeseen costs, and opens the door to a more stable financial future.

Creating Goals for Savings

A down payment on a house, a dream vacation, or an emergency fund are just a few examples of the kinds of goals that can spur you to save more regularly.

Emergency Reserve

Money put aside for unforeseen costs, such as medical bills, auto repairs, or job loss, is known as an emergency fund. Maintaining a minimum of three to six months' worth of living expenses in your emergency fund is advised.

Setting Up Auto-Savings

You should think about establishing automatic transfers from your checking to savings accounts. This guarantees that you set aside a portion of your earnings prior to making purchases.

Putting Money Into the Future

After you have accumulated a sizeable cushion of savings, think about investing your money to possibly earn higher returns. Several investment options, including stocks, bonds, and mutual funds, can be used to accomplish this.

In summary, having a solid understanding of banking and saving is essential for achieving financial success. Your financial future can be secured if you make saving a priority, manage your accounts carefully, and comprehend how banks operate. It's never too early to get started, and the financial habits you form now can benefit you for the rest of your life.

CHAPTER SIX

Making and Investing Money

The two main pillars of financial literacy are investing and earning. This chapter will cover the idea of earning money, the different sources of income, and how to invest wisely to get the most out of your hard-earned cash. Comprehending the fundamentals of earning and investing can assist anyone in reaching their financial objectives, be they an adult preparing for retirement or a teenager trying to save for a major purchase.

Making Money: Establishing a solid financial foundation begins with making money. It gives you the means to save for the future, pay for daily expenses, and make investments toward your long-term objectives. When it comes to making money, keep the following important ideas in mind:

Different Types of Income

a. Earned Income: This is money earned from a job or business. It includes your salary, wages, and any bonuses or commissions you may receive.

b. Passive Income: Passive income is income that is earned with little or no ongoing effort. It can come from investments, rental properties, or creative work royalties.

c. Portfolio income: This type of income is created by investments such as stocks, bonds, or mutual funds. It frequently includes capital gains and dividends.

Options for a Career

a. Your career choice has a significant impact on your earning potential. When deciding on a career path, keep your interests, skills, and education in mind.

b. To increase your earning potential, constantly improve your skills, pursue higher education, and explore opportunities for advancement.

Expenses and Budgeting

a. By keeping track of your spending and ensuring that you stay within your means, a budget helps you manage your income more skillfully.

b. Prioritize saving and investing some of your income over spending it on frivolous things.

Investing: The secret to gradually accumulating wealth is investing. You can take advantage of compound interest and reach your financial objectives by investing a portion of your income. Now let's explore the realm of investing:

The Value of Financial Investing

a. With time, investing helps your money grow, giving you the ability to outpace inflation and preserve or improve your purchasing power.

b. You can use investing to work toward retirement, financial independence, or certain financial objectives like home ownership or child education funding.

Vehicles for Investment

a. Stocks: Ownership shares in a company. They have the potential to provide both capital appreciation and dividends.

b. Bonds: Long-term debt securities that pay interest. It's often considered a lesser form of investment in comparison to stocks.

c. Mutual funds: Professional fund managers oversee money pools made up of contributions from numerous investors. They provide both professional expertise and diversification.

d. Real estate: Purchasing physical assets, like homes or businesses, can result in both capital growth and rental income.

e. Retirement Accounts: You can save money for retirement by using tax-advantaged accounts like IRAs and 401(k)s.

Diversification: To lower risk, diversify your investments by allocating your funds among several asset classes. Having a diverse portfolio will help you weather market swings.

Risk Tolerance: It's important to know how much risk you can take when investing. It chooses the combination of investments that best fits your comfort level and financial objectives.

Investing Techniques

a. Long-Term Investing: Make an effort to purchase and hold investments over time in order to take advantage of compounding.

b. Dollar-Cost Averaging: This technique can lessen the effects of market volatility by investing a set amount at regular intervals.

Monitoring and Modifying: To keep yourself on track with your financial objectives, periodically review your investment portfolio and make any necessary modifications.

In summary, financial literacy encompasses both earning and investing. You can strive for financial security and prosperity by learning how to optimize your income and make wise investment choices. Whether you're an adult saving for retirement or a teenager saving for your first car, it's never too early to start learning and applying these principles. Recall that knowledge and wise financial decisions are the first steps on the path to financial success.

CHAPTER SEVEN

Handling Credit and Debt

This chapter will examine the worlds of credit and debt, two vital financial instruments that can either help you or get you into financial difficulties. Many people have misconceptions about debt and credit, and ignorance can lead to expensive errors. You will understand exactly how to use these tools sensibly and responsibly by the end of this chapter.

Comprehending Debt

Debt is sums of money borrowed that have interest attached to them. It's an effective financial tool that can support you in reaching your objectives, including purchasing a home or vehicle, going to college, or launching a business. But it's important to understand the various forms of debt and how each operates.

Variety of Debt

1. Good Debt: Investing in your future is possible with good debt. This covers mortgages for homes or student loans for further education. Over time, these kinds of debt can assist in wealth accumulation.

2. Bad Debt: Bad debt is when you borrow money for items that depreciate over time, such as high-interest payday loans or credit card debt used for regular expenses. Prevent bad debt accumulation whenever feasible.

3. Consumer Debt: Credit card debt for non-essential purchases, auto loans, and personal loans fall under this category. Even though they have their uses, these must be handled with caution.

Managing Debts with Wisdom

Prior to incurring debt, take into account the following:

a. Interest Rates: Examine various interest rates and select the most affordable one. Reduced rates result in a cumulative reduction of interest paid.

b. Loan Terms: Recognize the conditions of your loan, such as the timetable for repayment and any early payment penalties.

c. Monthly Payments: Verify that you can pay your bills on time each month without going over your budget.

d. Emergency Fund: To avoid having to take on more debt, make sure you have an emergency fund set up to handle unforeseen costs.

e. Credit Score: Recognize that your credit score affects both the interest rates you will be offered and your ability to obtain loans. Your credit score will rise if you manage your debt responsibly and pay your bills on time.

Prudent Use of Credit

The ability to borrow money or use services now and pay for them later is known as credit. It's an important financial instrument, and handling it well can have a beneficial effect on your future financial situation.

Credit Cards

Credit cards are a popular type of credit and have a number of benefits and drawbacks.

The benefits of credit cards

a. Convenience: Credit cards are a handy tool for making purchases and are also useful in case of emergency.

b. Benefits: A lot of credit cards come with benefits like discounts, cashback, or travel points.

c. Credit Building: Using credit cards sensibly can contribute to a clean credit history.

Negative aspects of credit cards:

a. High-Interest Rates: Credit card interest rates can be extremely high if you have a balance.

b. Impulse Spending: If you're not careful, it's simple to overspend when using credit cards.

c. Fees: Annual fees, late payment fees, and other charges are frequently associated with credit cards.

Use Credit Cards Responsibly

You should heed the following advice in order to use credit cards responsibly:

a. To prevent incurring interest, pay off your balance in full each month.

b. To avoid going over budget, make a budget.

c. Reserve credit for anticipated or necessary purchases.

d. Keep an eye out for any unauthorized charges on your statements.

Establishing and Preserving Good Credit

For future financial opportunities, such as obtaining a mortgage or auto loan, a solid credit history is essential. You should pay attention to the following advice in order to establish and preserve good credit:

a. Always make on-time bill payments.

b. Maintain a small credit card balance to credit limit ratio.

c. Avoid making numerous credit applications at once as this may lower your credit score.

In summary, credit and debt are significant financial instruments that can result in financial difficulties or present opportunities. You can take charge of your financial future and lay the groundwork for a lifetime of financial success by being aware of the various forms of debt, managing it sensibly, and utilizing credit responsibly. You are ultimately responsible for your financial well-being, so make wise decisions.

CHAPTER EIGHT

Making Wise Financial Decisions

We've gone over key financial concepts like investing, saving, and budgeting in the previous chapters. It's time to start learning the art of wise financial decision-making. Numerous decisions in life have an impact on one's finances. Your current decisions will impact your financial future whether you're choosing how to spend your money, what to study in college, or whether to take out a loan. You will be walked through the process of making decisions that will put you on the road to financial success in this chapter.

Set Financial Goals

Establishing definite objectives is the first step toward making wise financial decisions. Finding the best course of action is difficult in the absence of goals. Consider the following:

1. What are my short-term and long-term financial objectives?

2. Should I buy a car, or a house, or save for retirement?

3. Which kind of life am I interested in leading?

4. What are my professional goals?

You can begin aligning your decisions with your goals once you've defined them. Knowing where you want to go will assist you in making decisions that will lead you in the right direction.

Recognize the Opportunity Cost

Every financial decision involves some sort of trade-off. It is critical to comprehend the concept of opportunity cost. The opportunity cost is what you forego when you choose one option over another. For example, if you decide to buy a new gaming console, the opportunity cost may be delaying your vacation savings. Consider the trade-offs and prioritize what is most important to you when making financial decisions.

Spend Your Money Wisely

A well-planned budget is your best tool for making sound financial decisions. Making a budget allows you to prioritize your spending and ensure you have enough money for essentials, savings, and fun. When budgeting, keep the following suggestions in mind:

1. Divide your expenses into categories such as housing, transportation, groceries, entertainment, and savings. This allows you to keep track of where your money is going.

2. Establish spending caps: Figure out how much you can afford to spend in each area, then adhere to that cap.

3. Save first: Before you spend money on anything else, set aside a portion of your income for savings. Make this a non-negotiable portion of your budget.

Avoid Buying on the Spot

Financial objectives can be severely harmed by impulsive purchases. It's tempting to buy something right away when you see something you want, but doing so frequently results in regret and overspending. To prevent impulsive purchases, follow the 24-hour rule. Prior to making any non-essential purchases, wait at least one day. This allows you time to consider it and see if it fits with your financial objectives.

Differentiating Needs from Wants

It's essential to distinguish between needs and wants in order to make wise financial decisions. Needs like food, shelter, and medical care are necessary for survival and overall health. Conversely, wants are items you can live without but still yearn for, such as the newest smartphone or high-end apparel. Set priorities for your needs and distribute your resources appropriately.

Make Research

Make sure you do your homework before making big financial decisions like investing, taking on debt, or picking a major in college. Examine your options, weigh the long-term effects of your decisions, and compare costs. When making decisions, get counsel from professionals and reliable sources.

Seek Advice

When making crucial financial decisions, don't be afraid to ask mentors, financial advisors, or other reliable adults for advice. They can share their experiences, offer insightful advice, and guide you through difficult decisions.

In conclusion, developing the ability to make wise financial decisions is a lifelong skill. Being knowledgeable and deliberate in your decisions is more important than trying to be flawless. Always remember to do your homework, identify needs from wants, budget sensibly, set clear goals, recognize opportunity costs, and, when needed, seek advice. You'll be in a better position to make decisions that result in security and prosperity in your finances if you adhere to these guidelines.

CHAPTER NINE

Financial Traps and How to Stay Away from Them

Achieving financial success requires knowing the potential financial pitfalls you may face, which is why money management is such an important life skill. This chapter will examine some typical financial pitfalls that young adults and teenagers encounter and offer helpful advice on how to steer clear of them.

1. Living Over Your Budget:

Overspending is a major financial trap that many people fall victim to. This may result in a difficult-to-break debt cycle. Take these precautions to stay away from this trap:

a. Establish a budget by listing your sources of income and outlays. Set aside some of your income for savings, and make sure that your out-of-pocket expenses don't outweigh your earnings.

b. Make a distinction between needs and wants: Give your needs — like a place to live, food, and transportation — priority over your wants — like going out to eat a lot or acquiring the newest technology.

c. Save and invest: Make it a habit to set aside money for both. You can create a safety net for unexpected expenses by setting aside a portion of your income for savings.

2. Abuse of Credit:

While credit cards can be a helpful tool for managing finances, improper use of them can result in debt. Avoid taking this risk by:

a. Recognize interest rates: Find out how interest rates on credit cards operate. Interest will be charged to your credit card account if you don't pay the entire balance each month. To avoid interest, make it a habit to pay off your credit card balance in full.

b. Use credit cards sensibly: Reserve them for urgent needs or necessary purchases. Do not overuse your credit cards or make impulsive purchases.

c. Credit monitoring: Make sure there are no mistakes or indications of identity theft by routinely reviewing your credit report.

3. Ignoring Savings for Emergencies:

Being without an emergency fund can be a serious financial mistake. Unexpected bills have the potential to put you in a tight spot financially. Avoid taking this risk by:

a. Establishing an emergency fund: Allocate a portion of your earnings towards the establishment of an emergency fund. Save up enough cash to last you for at least three or six months' worth of living expenses.

b. Setting savings as a top priority: Give saving money a top priority. Make an effort to save a little sum of money every month, even if you're paying off other debts or student loans.

4. Getting Wrenched in Debt:

A never-ending cycle of debt can result from payday loans, high-interest personal loans, and other predatory financial products. To steer clear of debt traps:

a. Exercise caution when taking out payday loans: Steer clear of these and other high-interest, quick-term loans. Look into other options, such as personal loans from respectable financial institutions, if you require financial assistance.

b. Speak with a financial advisor: To ensure that your decisions are well-informed, seek advice from a financial advisor if you're thinking about taking out a loan or already have debts.

5. Ignoring Long-Term Finance Objectives:

Long-term financial objectives like retirement planning are frequently disregarded by young adults. To evade this snag:

a. Begin saving for retirement early: Because of the power of compounding, the earlier you begin saving for retirement, the less you need to save each month. Contribute to your company's retirement plan (401(k)) and think about opening an Individual Retirement Account (IRA).

b. Diversify your investments: Do not put all of your money into one investment. To spread risk, diversify your portfolio.

c. Seek financial advice: Speak with a financial advisor to assist you in making wise decisions about your long-term financial goals.

In summary, your financial well-being depends on your ability to recognize and steer clear of financial pitfalls. You can lay a solid financial foundation for a prosperous future by managing your money wisely, recognizing needs from wants, and making wise financial decisions.

CHAPTER TEN

Creating Wealth and Reaching Financial Self-Sufficiency

We have already discussed the fundamentals of investing, saving, and budgeting in the earlier chapters. It's time to focus more on increasing wealth and obtaining financial independence at this point. Achieving financial success is a marathon that calls for meticulous preparation, self-control, and endurance. You will get the necessary information and techniques in this chapter to get you headed in the right direction.

The Capability of Compound Interest for Creating Wealth

Compound interest is one of the key ideas in wealth building. The way you use compound interest can either work in your favor or against you, like a magical force. Basically, it's the ability to earn interest on your initial investment as well as interest that accumulates over time. Over time, this compounding effect can greatly increase your savings and investments.

This straightforward example demonstrates the effectiveness of compound interest:

Assume you deposit $1,000 into a savings account with a 5% yearly interest rate. One year from now, you will have $1,050. However, in the second year, interest will be paid on the entire $1,050, not just the first $1,000. You are going to have $1,102.50 after two years. This snowball effect has the power to grow a small initial investment into a sizable sum over time.

To take advantage of compound interest to the fullest, start saving and investing early and consistently. Your money can work harder for you the longer you allow it to grow.

Investing to Increase Wealth

Although it won't make you wealthy, saving money in a bank account is a secure way to protect your wealth. Investing wisely is essential to achieving financial independence and building significant wealth. Here are some important investment choices to think about:

1. Stock Market: Purchasing stocks has the potential to generate large long-term gains. When you invest in a company, you become a shareholder, and your money grows as the company's value rises. Although it can be erratic, historically speaking, the stock market has produced strong returns over time.

2. Bonds: Bonds pay interest on a regular basis and are less risky than stocks. For investors who are more cautious, they make sense.

3. Real estate: Investing in real estate is a great way to accumulate wealth. If you own investment properties, you can earn rental income as real estate tends to appreciate over time.

4. Investment vehicles that let you diversify your holdings across a wide range of stocks and bonds are mutual funds and exchange-traded funds (ETFs). They're a fantastic option for novices.

5. Retirement Accounts: To save money for the future, make use of tax-advantaged retirement accounts like 401(k)s and IRAs. Contributions to these accounts grow tax-free or tax-deferred, which over time can greatly increase your wealth.

Managing Risk and Diversifying

One of the most important ways to lower risk in your investment portfolio is through diversification. It entails distributing your investments among several industries, geographical areas, and asset classes. You can avoid putting all your eggs in one basket by doing this. If one investment performs poorly, there may be others that outperform, protecting your wealth.

Having an emergency fund is another essential component of risk management. Having a safety net of funds will keep you from having to liquidate your investments in the event of a downturn, as unforeseen expenses can arise.

Ongoing Education and a Long-Term View

Achieving financial independence and building wealth takes a lifetime. Maintain your curiosity and keep learning about investing and personal finance. The state of the market will shift, and your financial objectives might too. It's critical to modify your tactics appropriately.

Recall that becoming wealthy quickly is not the goal of reaching financial independence. It all comes down to prudent investment choices, regular saving, and sound financial decision-making. You can create a solid financial foundation that will give you the flexibility and security to live your life as you see fit with enough time, patience, and discipline.

CHAPTER ELEVEN

Taking Charge of Your Future Financial Situation

You've arrived at the point in your financial literacy journey where you can take charge of your financial future. This chapter will walk you through the steps and strategies you'll need to take to secure your financial future and make informed decisions that will benefit you for years to come. It is critical to establish a solid financial foundation and develop good money habits as a teenager or young adult. Let's get this party started.

1. Establish Specific Financial Objectives

The first step in taking control of your financial future is to define your financial goals. What do you intend to use the money you're aiming to accumulate for? These objectives could include beginning a business, buying a car, moving out on your own, or even saving money for college. Establishing objectives that are precise, measurable, and attainable will provide you with a path to take and inspiration to continue on your current course.

2. Establish a Budget

Your financial plan, or budget, enables you to manage your spending while allocating your income to various needs and desires. First, make a note of all of your expenses and earnings. Make categories for discretionary spending on entertainment and non-essentials, as well as necessities like housing, food, transportation, and savings. Make an effort to live within your means by setting aside some cash every month. This process can be facilitated by the abundance of budgeting tools and applications that are available.

3. Establish a Reserve Account

Unexpected expenses can quickly throw off your financial plans because life is unpredictable. For this reason, setting up an emergency fund is essential. A high-yield savings account should have enough money saved in it to cover three to six months' worth of living expenses. When you most need financial stability and peace of mind, having an emergency fund in place can help.

4. Prudent Debt Management

It's critical to handle debt responsibly, whether it comes from credit card debt, auto loans, or education loans. Pay the minimum amount due on time, and if you can, try to pay less to lower the principal balance. Whenever possible, try to stay away from accruing high-interest debt. A critical component of taking charge of your financial future is realizing the costs associated with borrowing and the long-term effects of debt.

5. Make Long-Term Investments

One effective strategy for gradually increasing wealth is investing. Learn the fundamentals of investing first, as well as the different kinds of investments that are out there, like stocks, bonds, and mutual funds. If your employer offers a 401(k) or a Roth IRA, you should think about opening a retirement account. The power of compound interest can make your money grow if you invest regularly and at an early age.

6. Put Money Towards Education

Among the most important financial decisions you can make is to invest in yourself. Your education and abilities are assets that can lead to more lucrative employment prospects and improved earning capacity. Invest in your future and keep improving by allocating resources towards obtaining a college degree, vocational training, or certifications in your field.

7. Guard Your Resources

It's critical to safeguard your assets as you accumulate wealth and strive toward your financial objectives. This entails carrying health, auto, renters, house, and maybe life insurance coverage. Insurance acts as a safety net, assisting you in reducing the financial risks brought on by unplanned circumstances.

8. Keep Up Your Own Education

Developing financial literacy takes time. Keep up with changes to tax legislation, investment opportunities, and the financial industry. Go to seminars, read books, and keep up with reliable financial news sources. To assist you in making well-informed decisions regarding your investments, retirement planning, and tax strategies, you can also consult financial advisors.

In summary, taking charge of your financial future is a big step toward reaching your life goals and ensuring your financial well-being. You'll be well on your way to financial success if you set specific goals, make a budget, save, make smart investments, and never stop learning. Keep in mind that achieving financial freedom is a journey rather than a destination, so remain dedicated to making wise financial decisions for the rest of your life. You'll be grateful to yourself in the future.

CONCLUSION

'Financial Literacy for Teens and Young Adults' is an invaluable tool for people starting their path to security and financial independence. We have covered the fundamentals of money management, decision-making, and laying a solid financial foundation throughout this book. Young readers have given themselves the knowledge and abilities needed to successfully negotiate the complicated world of personal finance by developing a thorough understanding of budgeting, saving, investing, and avoiding typical financial pitfalls.

As we come to the end of this educational journey, it is important to stress that financial literacy is a key to unlocking a better future, not just a matter of math and statistics. The lessons found in these pages go far beyond money management; they are instruments for realizing goals, ensuring one's own safety, and contributing to society. By keeping these ideas in mind, teenagers and young adults can take charge of their financial future, make plans for unforeseen expenses, and embark on a journey toward financial independence.

It is our hope that this book's insights and strategies have not only made readers more knowledgeable, but also inspired a lifelong interest in finance and a dedication to lifelong learning. The knowledge gained here will be extremely valuable in a world where financial opportunities and challenges are constant. Young adults can reap the benefits of financial independence, make wise decisions, and advance their personal and professional lives by putting these lessons into practice and modifying them to fit their evolving situations.